DIVORCING
The GAME

DIVORCING The GAME

MOVING TOWARD YOUR TRUE PURPOSE

VICTOR HOBSON

DIVORCING THE GAME
MOVING TOWARD YOUR TRUE PURPOSE

iUniverse books may be ordered through booksellers or by contacting:

*iUniverse
1663 Liberty Drive
Bloomington, IN 47403
www.iuniverse.com
1-800-Authors (1-800-288-4677)*

ISBN: 978-1-4917-9966-6 (sc)
ISBN: 978-1-4917-9967-3 (e)

Library of Congress Control Number: 2016909578

Print information available on the last page.

iUniverse rev. date: 08/05/2016

CONTENTS

PREFACE

In 2003, I stepped onto the field of my dreams, and life as I had hoped began to unfold. Having graduated from the University of Michigan and been drafted to play for the New York Jets, I knew this was the beginning of great things for me. Big dreams—yes, I had them, and they were finally beginning to manifest. Football had always been my passion, something I loved to do. So an opportunity to play professionally was definitely high on my bucket list. Little did I realize in 2003 that football would just place me on the path to greatness and on a journey to discover my true purpose.

The goal in life is not to be defined by what you do. The real goal is to establish what you do and to use that as a platform to do even greater things in life. That is the true game. The game I played was just a stepping-stone to a future of unlimited opportunities. The higher we go in life, the more we can achieve and the more we discover. Sometimes we reach one of our dreams, manifesting one of our heart's desires, or we quench the thirst in life and get stuck, believing "this is as good as it gets."

Oftentimes we allow one victory to overshadow our true purpose, and we settle with accomplishing one goal, winning one victory, manifesting one dream. But on this journey, I discovered a golden nugget: what you're willing to walk away from determines what you walk into. The void that opens creates the space for what you desire.

Divorcing the Game is a journey toward self-discovery. Although the principles may be presented from a locker-room, athletic, on-the-field perspective, the ideals and beliefs spill over into the game of life. Discovering who you are, finding your purpose, and being the best you can be in this life is the object of the game. The manifestation of such equals victory!

Never settle for good when better is out there waiting for you. Divorce anything that limits your view, blocks your true purpose, or causes you to think that without it, you will fail. Open your mind to the unlimited opportunities that God has placed on the earth just for you. Celebrate each stop on the journey, but don't settle there. When one door closes, keep an eye out for the next open door. A closed door doesn't mean that it's over. It only means that a greater opportunity awaits you on the other side. Keep moving forward. Keep striving to do better. Keep reaching for the top. You were built to win!

ACKNOWLEDGMENTS

To all the people who have come across my path and knowingly or unknowingly made me a better person. To my wife for being a pillar by my side. To my mother and father for sacrificing themselves to provide me better opportunities. To my grandmother and grandfather, who were my greatest fans. To my children, who see me through their innocent eyes as the perfect man who I am not but who I strive to be, because of my love for them. To my mentors who have opened my eyes to see a new realm of who I was created to be and what I was created to achieve in this world. I thank everyone who told me what I wasn't and what I could never do for indirectly helping me to work harder to achieve what I have done and the greater accomplishments that I plan to do.

First Quarter

INTRODUCTION

Obstacles don't have to stop you.
If you run into a wall, don't turn around and give up.
Figure out how to climb it, go through it, or work around it.
—Michael Jordan

There comes a point in all our lives when we have to let go of something we love (a loved one, a career, a pet, a favorite car). It's inevitable in this world that we live in, and it's something that the universe doesn't seem to compromise on. How we deal with adversity and with the devastation of losing something or someone we love reveals the character that has been instilled in us throughout our lives. The trials and tribulations we encounter are intricate pieces of life's puzzle, used in developing the character that we must have to succeed.

There is no school or class in the world that can prepare you for the unexpected loss of something you love. Experience is the best teacher. When my beloved grandmother, whom I loved with all my heart, died in my arms after a long hard fight with cancer. The reality set in that I would never see her again. There was nothing in this world that could prepare me for how I would react to such a devastating loss. Would I fall into a state of depression because I no longer had one of my inspirational forces with me, or would I adapt to the changes that the universe dealt me and use the priceless inspirational lessons that my grandmother had taught me to honor her with my success? The choice for me was easy.

That experience didn't compare to the day that I gave 100 percent of my energy to a team, believing that there was no way I would *not* be a part of that team. The contributions that I was providing were too great for me not to be on the team, in my opinion. But those feelings were not mutual, and I was told, "Thanks for what you have done for us, however we are going in a different direction."

What do you do when the movie that you've been starring in for the majority of your life is cut short? When a portion of the masculinity you've intertwined into a game and identified with is left on the desk where you gave the coach your final handshake, solidifying that your playing career is finished?

The choices we make when faced with adversity go a long way in determining the legacies we leave our children and families to enjoy and the rest of the world to remember. In fact, these choices are all about character, separating average from exceptional. One of the most important lessons I learned in playing sports was that it doesn't matter how you start something; what matters is how you finish. In most instances, it's easiest to develop a game plan for your postcareer success while you're in the height of your career. You then can immediately begin to execute that game plan when the time presents itself, if all factors remain favorable. The problem arises when adversity boldly presents itself in your life and you're forced to change the game plan that you so carefully calculated.

Success comes with the ability to adapt to any situation with the fortitude and will to execute your game plan and bring your dreams and goals to full fruition. These assets allow you to leave a legacy for your children and family to continue and for the world to admire and benefit from. We polled a group of athletes, asking, "If the game you love was taken from you, would you be successful in another profession?" One hundred percent responded in the affirmative, without hesitation. However, that's easier said than done.

Many athletes who are blindsided by career-ending injuries or removed from teams without prior warning find it very difficult to make the transition from the game on the field or on the court to the game of life. We will tackle these issues as we explore my life as I divorced the game on the field and discovered and embraced a life of unlimited possibilities and opportunities—dreaming bigger, reaching higher, manifesting my true purpose, and embracing every minute of it.

Chapter 1

Divorce Is Not an Option

Your Future Is in Your Hands

"I'm still in my prime."

"They just don't have the right system for my skills."

"Some team will pick me up soon."

"I'm better than him. Why would they want to keep him on the team instead of me?"

"I got caught up in the politics of the game; otherwise, I would still be playing."

"My agent didn't do a good job of getting my name out there."

"The coach just didn't like me."

These are the sentiments of athletes who's careers are ending or have abruptly ended. It's perfectly reasonable to have a complex mix of emotions and thoughts running through your mind upon reaching such a critical juncture. You feel like you've been robbed. The career you've put your heart and soul into is taken away from you, and you're in a fighting mood. You've devoted your entire life to a sport, and now you're expected to just give it all up. Of course, you're angry; it's only natural. One thing is certain: you want to find someone or something to blame for it.

Game Rule #1
Don't allow outside forces to dictate your future.

As with most angry reactions, fear is a catalyst. This is a new situation that you're dealing with, and you don't know how to handle it. What are you going to do now that the rest of your life has changed? Why can't you stop playing the game on *your* terms? You know you aren't being realistic. But raw emotions aren't about being realistic; they just happen. It's a sign of how passionate you've always been about the sport that you love so much.

Never allow anger or the negative effects of the blame game to overtake your mind. Don't allow outside forces to dictate your future. The sooner you come to the realization that everyone else is not the enemy, the better off you'll be. This would be a great opportunity to stop and reevaluate your inner man (the "inner me") to ensure that he isn't the real enemy. You're the owner of your own entity (which is you).

You have to love and respect yourself more than you love the game. Many athletes pour their hearts, minds, bodies, and souls into perfecting the skills of the game, only to realize that the game had never been loyal to anyone. As soon as another opportunity presents itself (someone younger, faster, and stronger), the game will divorce you and marry him. You will find yourself on the outside looking in.

Athletes are trained their entire careers to conquer by any means necessary and never to give up, but how do they gauge when the very thing to which they have given their all and have fought so hard for has moved on?

Opportunity or Failure: You Decide

Game Rule #2
Opportunity often comes disguised as failure.

The longer you hold on to something that is not holding on to you, the greater your chances of missing considerable opportunities to transition in your career. Opportunity often comes disguised as failure. The powers that be may conclude that you're no longer what the game wants, but if you believe that you're still in your prime and you're better than everyone else in your position, then prove it. Yet also remember that your sport is the stepping-stone to your future, and that future will come sooner rather than later. I'm still searching for an athlete who retired from his sport at sixty-five.

A true competitor competes off the field as well as on the field. He competes just as hard in the game of life as he does on the playing field. He acquires the skills to succeed in life through his experiences in the sport. The game shouldn't dictate what an athlete competes for, because in the long run he will fail. The problem arises when the athlete believes that the game justifies who he is as a person. The game is just a tool to help enhance and sharpen the person you are inside, the real you. As soon as you understand this about yourself, you can truly thank the game for what it has done for you as a person and strive to be successful in what you choose to do in the future.

Game Rule #3
Actively plan for the future while still in your present.

There's a thin line between feeling like you want to give up and knowing when to let go and move on. The person that can distinguish the difference between the two will ultimately be successful. Distress signals go off in a competitor's mind when he isn't able to finish on his own terms. Sadly, those terms are often undefined. He may have never had a definite plan for the number of years he wanted to play in the game or how he wanted his career to end. One of my spiritual advisers once told me that no one plans to fail, but many people fail to plan.

Why is it so disappointing when the game ends your career without your input, without your consent, and without your acknowledgment that you're ready to stop? Did you plan on playing the game forever? Did you actively plan to do something else in life? Or did you think you would always be in control and could walk away from the game when you felt it was appropriate? Only a very small percentage of athletes are blessed with the opportunity to use the game for everything that they can get out of it and then walk away on their own terms and even then I often wonder if the risk outweighed the reward.

You have to understand that letting go of the game doesn't equal giving up. I don't believe in divorce, but in this case, legal separation is an option. Take what you've learned from the game and use it to propel you into the successful future that's awaiting you. Don't allow the game to hold you hostage; don't reach for something that has left you behind. You increase the risk of becoming a statistic for someone else's future.

As the game gets bigger, it gets faster. The speed of your career within the sport increases as well. In other words, your mind and body must adapt to the accelerated rate of life after the game. Now, I'm not suggesting that you give less than 100 percent to the game. Any time you don't give your all to the endeavor at which you're attempting to succeed, you not only prevent yourself from benefiting others, but you cheat yourself out of opportunity as well. You have to have a viable, consistent, and effective transition plan that benefits those connected to your success but also includes a plan for you to transition into the rest of your life without holding on to the former thing. Let the past stay in the past. Allow the former thing, although it was successful, to stay in the past as you move forward into a brighter, more fulfilling future.

Game Rule #4
Let the past stay in the past.

Overcoming Fear

Never let the fear of striking out get in your way.
—Babe Ruth

Fear is one of the most difficult emotions to overcome when letting go of something you love. There's a thin line between letting go and holding on just long enough that you miss a great opportunity. Fear is a thief of great opportunity. Many great men have forfeited their destiny as a result of fear of the unknown. Author Marianne Williamson describes it best: "Our deepest fear is not that we are inadequate. Our deepest fear is that we are powerful beyond measure." Fear of the unknown has defeated many great men.

Many people have never had the chance to discover they were great, because fear stole their opportunity to pursue their true greatness. Many athletes have achieved greatness in their particular sport or at least were considered among the elite in the game. However, their greatness on the field was overshadowed because their achievements there were superseded by their lack of accomplishments off the field.

Game Rule #5
Fear is a thief of great opportunity.

Your occupational title of "athlete" doesn't define your true self. Your sport grants you only the opportunity to make a name for yourself in the eyes of the public. It's a stepping-stone to your future life after the game. Your perspective on leaving the game then becomes one of transition not divorce; it is a positive change, not a negative one. Since the game itself has never had a problem moving on and definitely doesn't show any emotions, the player is left holding a bag of hurt, disappointment, and loss. As the old saying goes, "Here today, gone tomorrow."

A positive transition, as opposed to a negative divorce, allows you to transition from one career to another smoothly, with the athlete hopefully understanding the benefits gained and using them as a springboard into a bright future. The key is not to allow fear to force you into a divorce from your sport. Allow your sport to prepare you to transition into your destiny. Fear will leave you holding on to a game that has remarried and abandoned you to the winds of self-destruction. "For as a man thinks in his heart so is he" (Proverbs 23:7).

Life is all about learning from yesterday, living for today, and hoping for tomorrow.
—*Albert Einstein*

The Defeat of Divorce

There is no such thing as a smooth divorce. Disappointment and hurt are always the result for one or both parties. Divorce is an ugly word and not one usually associated with sports. The time an athlete dedicates to his sport sometimes outweighs the time and effort he dedicates to his real marriage. Sadly enough, I was probably guilty of that at one point in my life. Not every athlete is married, and those who aren't married surely understand this dilemma when the blessing of marriage presents itself.

In essence, you spend a large part of your day perfecting your craft, working toward something that has never been accomplished in the history of sports, yet something that's still very much expected every time you step onto the playing field. At the end of the day, you realize that you're married to the game that you love. You're loyal to the game because it's fun and has paved the way for you to obtain a lifestyle unlike any other you've seen.

Game Rule #6
Time waits for no one.

When you reach the end of the road in the sport that you love, you have three options: (1) Capitalize on your accomplishments and on the relationships that you've established throughout your marriage to the game, which gives you the ability to transition smoothly into the game of life. (2) Keep fighting for your marriage to the game, and pray that the game you love so dearly can rekindle the love you felt it once had for you. Caution: This option has a very low success rate. The fact is, the game loves youth, and time waits for no one. As you get older and wiser, the game has one eye on you and another on prospects in the shadows, waiting for their opportunity. (3) Choose to end your marriage to the game. In essence, divorce the game. This is somewhat similar to fighting for your marriage, and nothing in a divorce is pretty. Somebody has to assume the blame.

You feel like your team doesn't want you or appreciate you, but you believe that you can go on a date with another team and possibly find a connection there. You have to fire your agent, because he doesn't have the connections that you feel he should have (even though he helped you sign your contract with your first team). You tell everyone how bad the coach is, but in reality you probably don't understand how to respect authority. You complain that you're better than the person for whom your team released you, but why didn't another team immediately sign you?

Outwardly you cry out because you're hurt, while internally you fight to hold on to something that nine times out of ten has already moved on and remarried. Now, there's a slim chance that the game will reach back for you and rekindle the relationship. But, realistically, how long will that last? At that point, is it a rekindled marriage or is it just a lust for the familiar?

Game Rule #7
Allow your past to catapult you into a greater future.

Understanding how to embrace the inevitable obstacles that will present themselves is predicated on knowing who you are. When you know who you are, you're able to understand and avoid the obstacles that are thrown your way. Not only do you have to know who you are, but you also have to listen to and understand your inner self, the "sixth sense" that we often hear about. When you acknowledge and follow the voice of your inner self, you will know when it's time to move on and pursue other ventures, adventures, and opportunities.

This is the game of life. When you play the game according to these rules, people say you have good instincts. The instincts you developed over time that led you to making big plays and thinking fast on your feet will help you transition from the game on the field to the game of life.

Feeling sorry for yourself not only allows time to pass you by, but also keeps you stuck in a place that doesn't let you progress in life. Progression is a natural part of the universe. The universe is never standing still. Likewise, you must continue to move forward. A coach used to always tell me, "If you don't get better, you get worse; and if you stay the same, you get worse also." Progression denotes success, and success is continually moving forward, not holding on to the things of the past. Progression is utilizing the sport of your past to catapult you into a greater future.

Chapter 2

The Transition

Times of transition are strenuous, but I love them. They are an opportunity to purge, rethink priorities, and be intentional about new habits. We can make our new normal any way we want. —*Kristin Armstrong*

Don't Miss Your Opportunity

One of the most difficult tasks for athletes is to transition from the sport that they love so dearly into another area of their passion. Where that transitional period will lead and how long it will last is completely up to the individual. After devoting the majority of your life to a career, it's normal to take time to identify and develop your new passion. However, it's very easy to miss a new opportunity if you hold on to the past.

Although missing one opportunity doesn't mean you've forfeited your future, it does mean you have to wait until the next opportunity presents itself to you. Opportunities come and go; that's a part of the cycle of life. However, it's up to you to decipher between true opportunities and distractions. Distractions can make your transition just as difficult as it would be if you held on to your past.

Game Rule #8
Failure is permanent only if you give up.

Transition can be defined as the pivotal point in your life when you catapult yourself into your destiny. Transition is not easy. The fact that you want to be successful after you're finished playing doesn't automatically translate into success. The same desire, intensity, focus, and determination that it took to establish your name in your sport is needed to reestablish yourself on your new field of life.

There is no guarantee that you will be successful at every endeavor. However, if you fail at your next endeavor, failure is only permanent if you give up. You must find the field of your dreams that you can turn into your "home stadium" and receive the same cheers that you used to receive when playing your sport. If you start to feel like you have the home field advantage, you've probably transitioned successfully into a new career.

Game Rule #9
Anything that remains stagnant will eventually spoil.

A key element in transitioning from one career to the next is accepting that it's time for change and that change doesn't mean you're giving up on your sport. If you aren't given the opportunity to leave the sport on your own terms, it doesn't mean you've forsaken the goals you originally set. It does mean you aren't allowing yourself to remain stagnant in a dead situation. Anything that remains stagnant eventually spoils. The time it takes to accept that a change is necessary has a significant impact on how long it takes you to transition into a new career.

Pride: Let It Go!

Pride greatly affects an athlete's ability to change. When you're dealing with top-level athletes, pride is a major component. It's difficult for a prideful athlete to let go of the perks that catered to his ego during and even after his gladiator days. The constant attention we receive, the focus on our exceptional skill level—even if to a certain extent we don't always like to be under the microscope, it is easy to miss when it's no longer there.

Fans patting you on the back, reporters asking for quotes, and the chase for the next big contract all feed our ego and fill us with pride, and rightfully so! We have put in years and years of blood, sweat, and tears. You recall the hard work, determination, dedication, and focus that it took for you to become a professional athlete. When other guys were out having fun and enjoying themselves, you were practicing, training, and building up your mind and body. Then there were all the injuries, the pain, and the endless rehab; like a warrior, you fought your way through it. Naturally, pride comes with the territory.

However, when your playing days are over, reality sets in, and your ego begins to whisper in your ear that you may not be accepted in society the same as you were when you were playing your sport. You may not like it, but humility is forced upon you. The reality is that the sport never determined your identity. Your ego paints a picture that can severely distort your understanding of reality. Even if you feel as if you have plenty of good reasons to feel prideful, pride is like playing with fire. The Bible says that pride comes before a fall. Don't allow the perception created by your ego to alter the reality of your limitations. When you accept and embrace your reality, you can transition into anything that you choose, at a pace you control.

Game Rule #10
Do not allow the perception created by your ego to alter the reality of your limitations.

Everything Must Change. Embrace It!

Control has a lot to do with accepting change. When people can dictate the change happening in their lives, they are more receptive to it. Therefore, be very clear in your own mind that you're going to seize control of the transition. After all, it's your life. To best control the changes in your transition period, have a definitive plan and a vision that allows you to shift gears smoothly into your future. As a proverb says, "A plan without a vision is considered daydreaming, but a vision without a plan will be a nightmare." Either way you look at it, there's no way around the fact that you must both dictate a smooth transition and control the pace of the change that occurs.

Athletes that have been able to transition immediately into another career were prepared for the end of their sports career well before they received notice of that end. Preparing psychologically for the end before you get there is not easy, because it feels like you're speaking death into your career before it's over. I would never talk about what I would do after I was done playing football, because I thought I would be playing forever, or at least until I chose to say I was done. I always knew that I was a lot bigger than what I could offer through football, but I didn't want to accept that I would need a backup plan to prove it.

Game Rule #11
The game waits for no one.

Young athletes who have made their way into professional sports often consider themselves invincible. You can preach all you want about a what-if plan, but reality usually has to hit them in the face before they understand that playing sports is not life. Playing a professional sport allows you to provide a better life for you and your family. But all it takes is one injury for a young athlete to realize that the game waits for no one. Just because you aren't able to play doesn't mean that the league and your team stops moving forward.

Lloyd Carr, former coach at the University of Michigan, used to tell us as a team that "expectation is for the position." In essence, he was preparing us for the cold but ever-so-present truth that the expectation is the same for whoever puts on a jersey and steps onto the field in any given position. It doesn't matter who you are or what you've done in the past. The game is loyal to whoever is the best at filling one of the eleven positions on the football field. If you're unable to perform, nothing will stop the game from moving on without you.

No athlete has been able to retire at age sixty-five. Therefore, the need to transition into something after your career ends is obvious. No matter how long you've been able to play, once your playing career ends, you still have a large part of your life to pursue other passions and dreams. Don't allow yourself to be like many professional athletes, who started to pay attention to the obvious when it was too late. I could go on and recite the horror stories of professional athletes who didn't prepare for life after sports and even abused the opportunities they had, but I don't want to engage in scare tactics.

Game Rule #12
Anything that performs according to its purpose will eventually die.

We have all heard stories of athletes who turned their lives into a train wreck, both personally and financially, by not honoring the fact that an athlete's playing days have a limited shelf life. Granted, the length of time varies from one athlete to another, but the actual date your playing career ends is not important. The fact is that your playing career will come to an end one day, and you must be well prepared. The sad part is that that day always seems to come sooner than we expect.

There is no reason a professional athlete's career end has to become another tragic story. Not having a plan or at least a vision of what you would like to do when your career ends can leave you in a desperate situation. The universe is in a constant state of progression. Therefore, everything living must evolve and grow with it, or it will be left behind.

Death is inevitable. I'm not referring to a physical death, but a psychological death that occurs when we fail to evolve. If you remain stagnant and fail to move forward in your life, you will stop progressing and innovating. Anything that performs according to its purpose will eventually die, especially your mind.

Avoiding the Desperate

An inability to transition effectively after your professional career will eventually affect your finances. The money you worked so hard to earn during your career will begin to deplete, throwing you into a state of desperation. Desperation is the result of poor choices and ultimately leads to fear and stagnation. You find yourself in a catch-22: your finances are depleting and you're standing still, unable to move forward into another arena.

Eventually something has to give. It usually starts with your lifestyle and then trickles down. The luxuries you've accumulated become a target, and you begin to downsize. Suddenly, you're desperate, looking for any job that can keep you halfway afloat. Desperation leads to emotional decisions, which ultimately cause you to question the decisions you initially made.

Game Rule #13
Change presents itself with or without your permission.

Desperation causes people to go into survival mode. It's hidden within anyone that feels as if his back is against the wall. In survival mode, people live according to the survival of the fittest; they will do anything to survive and provide for themselves or their family. Oftentimes, desperate measures lead to moral debates within them, and sometimes morality loses. When morality wins, humiliation sets in, and you end up at a job that you aren't happy with. Regret is usually the result, as you realize that it didn't have to be that way. However, it's never too late to change. Why live life filled with regrets?

Transition is inevitable, no matter who you are or what you do for a living. You can attempt to avoid it or pretend that it isn't there, but eventually you'll find yourself faced with it. Change presents itself in your life and in your experience with or without your permission.

Change will not come if we wait for some other person or some other time.
We are the ones we've been waiting for. We are the change that we seek.
—*Barack Obama*

As a man, you must choose to embrace the change and use it as a transitional boost toward your future. You can also choose to resist the change and watch as a transition takes place, leaving you in an eventual state of playing catch-up as you try to redeem the time you lost.

Game Rule #14
Within transition lies an opportunity for you to capitalize on your greatness.

It's true that not all change is in your best interest. However, that doesn't alter the fact that change has to take place at some point in your life. With a plan and a keen understanding of who you are as a person and of your ultimate purpose, you can recognize the true opportunities to transition into your future.

Transition can be one of the most uncomfortable stages in your life, but that doesn't necessarily mean it's a bad thing. In fact, it's usually the opposite. It's through uncomfortable times that a person is able to discover his true being and his hidden gifts and talents that can truly make him successful.

> *But we have this treasure in earthen vessels, that the excellency*
> *of the power may be of God, and not of us.*
> *—2 Corinthians 4:7*

No one likes to be uncomfortable. When a person is uncomfortable, it's natural for him to move around to find a comfortable position. Just think of how irritated an oyster is when a piece of sand invades its little shell. That discomfort forces it to adjust. The result is an adjustment that births a beauty of nature that many desire: a natural pearl.

Change is God's way of moving you out of your comfort zone so you search within yourself to discover the hidden pearls. In transition lies an opportunity for you to capitalize on your greatness. Discomfort gives you the choice to either embrace the change or run from it.

> *Progress is impossible without change, and those who*
> *can't change their minds can't change anything.*
> *George Bernard Shaw*

Second Quarter

Chapter 3

Becoming the Rule, Not the Exception

When purpose is not known, abuse is inevitable.
—Myles Monroe

Don't Become a Statistic

Don't allow yourself to become a statistic of the game. Many men have great potential; the problem arises when their potential isn't met. In professional sports, athletes strive to break records. I quietly went after most of them myself. Yet some statistics reflect failure, not achievement.

Two statistics are sadly but commonly achieved by athletes and rarely, if ever, celebrated. The first is this: over 50 percent of professional athletes' marriages end in divorce. The other is that an overwhelming number of professional athletes faced financial hardship after their professional careers end. Both of these statistics are close to my heart, because I am married and understand the work that goes into making a marriage prosper and because I was one of the athletes who was headed into financial hardship. The choices I was making and not making caused me to hop on a direct route toward bankruptcy.

The lack of perameters that I had set for myself and refused to be accountable to allowed me to perceive I was doing everything right, and the statistic I assumed I would never be a part of lingered around me like a black hole with no way out. Fortunately, the right team of people surrounded me, the most important being my now wife. It was my first experience in understanding I didn't have to live with the rule; I could choose to become the exception. I learned that life is a journey and that my outlook on journey would prove to be my destruction or my destiny.

How do you explain to anyone that he has wasted more money than a lot of people make in their lifetime? For a minute I forgot my self-worth, but I made a decision to disassociate myself from what I was not and focus on the fact that I had always worked to become a great success. Not until I stopped being embarrassed about where my choices led me could I stare my situation in the face. I had to look bankruptcy in the face and say, "You are not the definition of me. I am the captain of this ship, and I sail only toward greatness."

You can either make statistics or become a part of the statistics. Most statistics aren't team accomplishments. They are individual awards at the end of the day. So if you become a statistic, don't expect anyone to take responsibility for you in your downhill slide. You either become the rule, which in most cases states that the game breaks you, or you become the exception, and you break the game.

The Marriage Dilemma

Love is patient, love is kind. It doesn't envy, it doesn't boast, it is not proud. It doesn't dishonor others, it is not self-seeking, it is not easily angered, it keeps no record of wrongs. Love doesn't delight in evil but rejoices with the truth. It always protects, always trusts, always hopes, always perseveres. Love never fails.
—1 Corinthians 13:4–8

An alarming 60 to 80 percent of marriages in the NFL end in divorce. What a heartbreaking statistic! The majority of these divorces happen after the athlete's peak earning period has ended and he has retired. Why? Truthfully, I don't know why, and I'm not going to speculate. What I will do is tell you what marriage is and why football should be one of the best preparations for it.

This is an extremely hard chapter for me to write, because I feel like a hypocrite, knowing my own marriage isn't perfect. What I do know is that my wife and I are a team. If you ask me what the perfect marriage is, I don't have an answer. I do know what commitment is, and through all of my mistakes I still strive to be a better man, husband, and father. I am not writing as a saint whose walk is flawless. I profess to be a gladiator in spirit who understands that every day is a fight to become the best on my all-pro home team.

Game Rule #15
The bigger the storm, the greater the victory.

The bigger the storm the greater the victory. The bigger the struggle the further your progress. It's inevitable that teams go through bad stretches. Adversity defines a team and allows the audience to see how they react to adversity and how they handle pressure. It is there that true character is exposed. Does adversity tear them apart and cause them to blame each other for the mistakes, challenges, or mishaps, or does it draw them closer together and allow them to be one of the greatest teams striving toward a dynasty?

As athletes, we play team sports in some aspect of our lives. And, as men, we should understand that the best team that God can give us is a family. No team in the world can surpass or even compete with the team that God joins together. What good is a man who gains all the success in the world on the field, but fails with his home team: his wife and children? That failure transforms you from being the athlete or the coach into being a spectator in your own house. No man ever wants to reach the point where he has to buy a ticket to see his own family.

Your family is your all-pro team. Why would you want to destroy it? Everyone should be cheering when they see the way you function as a family and possibly booing at your mistakes.

What if the marriage that everyone seems to think is all about them is not about the individuals at all? Marriage has to be about love. Love makes you a servant to someone else. Love can't be selfish. Otherwise, it's called lust, not love. Some couples may go through the motions and rituals of marriage (the ceremony, vows, etc.) but may not be in love or may not understand the words of their vows.

Game Rule #16
Successful marriages are built on teamwork.

Marriage is work. You encounter situations and challenges that you've never had to face or endure. You tolerate things that you've never had to tolerate. You realize that you have to look to God to learn how to become a better husband. This eventually leads you to develop a stronger relationship with Him. What if, in the overall big picture of life, God used marriage to create a stronger, more intimate relationship between a man and a woman? I'm not saying that all marriages are meant to be or meant to last. But if you don't understand the institution of marriage, your self is in control. Successful marriages are built only on teamwork. Selfishness has no part on the team.

The Money Dilemma

In 2009 Sports Illustrated issued a study saying an alarming 78 percent of NFL players were in financial hardship or filed for bankruptcy two years after their professional careers ended. Similarly, 60 percent of NBA players were in financial hardship five years after their careers. These figures are truly staggering, and they shatter the public's perception of the professional athlete's life.

Many people think professional athletes just ride off into the sunset after their careers end. They believe professional athletes are set for life and can sit around and do not much of anything for the rest of their lives, if that's what they choose. I came into the NFL with the same misconception.

Misunderstanding the value of money is the easiest way to discover that money is a lot harder to make than it is to spend. Money comes and goes, as with everything in the world. However, it's a long fall from grace when you don't have any savings to pad the fall. That fall from grace is the sad reality of many professional athletes.

The question is, how and why do so many athletes who were once on top of the world fall victim to this? Who can you blame? Can you blame anyone at all? There is plenty of blame to go around, but at the end of the day, the one that must be held accountable is the athlete. I say this not to insinuate that no one will take advantage of you or that people don't make mistakes. Both most certainly do happen and far too frequently. Instead, that makes up a small percentage of the reasons so many athletes end up broke, lost in the financial shuffle. It starts with the mentality of the athlete.

No one can avoid being a statistic without understanding the business of the game. I used the word *business*, because any time money is being transferred for your services, that is a business transaction, not a game. The game is the sport itself, but the business is your day-to-day interactions within that game. What you provide for the fans is a beautiful game. What you do in that game to provide for yourself and your family is your business. Once you transition from college to professional, you're catapulted into the real world of business. Unless you understand the business that you're walking into, you will be shocked by everything that comes your way.

Game Rule #17
How you play on the field determines how well you live off the field.

We spend a large portion of our lives developing our God-given gifts, playing the game we love, and entertaining the masses. We're programmed to conquer everything on the field of play. Little do you know that once your status changes to professional, your play on the field determines how well you live off the field, and how you live off the field determines how well you live in the future.

A lot of players hear what the NFL stands for and the ins and outs of the business, but very few comprehend those facts. They're too busy developing their on-field expertise and basking in the glory days of their careers. When I began my professional career, I was told that NFL stands for Not For Long. But that didn't mean anything to me or to any of the other high draft picks. We assumed we could control the cards the game dealt. We thought we could move mountains. We had the world at our feet. Why worry about some future day that seemed so remote that we felt like it would never come?

This is where understanding the football business becomes pivotal to your future success. The average career life of a football player is 3.3 years. That means that if you're finished playing football in college at age twenty-one, or twenty-two at the latest, your football career is over by the time you're twenty-five. Let's say that you are above the average and play for ten years. This still puts you at thirty-two years old, with a large portion of your life still in front of you.

You spend years preparing for something that's over before you've lived even half of your life. This is the most important fact to grasp when embarking on a career that can potentially establish you financially for the rest of your life. But this is the hardest concept to fathom when you're young and feel like you're invincible. Understanding this point is pivotal to how much you value the game and all that comes with it.

A lot of coaches tell us to play every play like it is our last. That may be a good approach to the game, but what would happen if you took that approach with each of your paychecks as well? Would you spend so freely? Would you trust everyone wearing a nice suit and driving a fancy car who says they can make you more money? Would you invest in anything that sounds good without getting the proper advice first? Would you be lackadaisical in reviewing your financial statements?

When there's a sense of urgency, human instinct naturally kicks in and we increase the efficiency in which we handle daily responsibilities. That sense of urgency is a mentality that needs to become a habit as you handle your finances. You are human. Nothing can stop you from making mistakes. However, the lessons you learn from your mistakes play a big role in your financial future.

As a young athlete, I wasn't prepared to create wealth through the opportunities I was being granted as a football player. There was no structure to what or why I was spending money, and I had no clear-cut plan for attaining financial success. It's easy for me to say that I had a bad financial adviser who didn't sit me down and explain everything to me. However, at the end of the day, how can someone get me to do what my mind wasn't prepared to do? I should have truly entertained the meetings with my advisors and strategized for my financial future. I had goals for the football field, and even if I didn't achieve them all, I always had something to shoot for. As the saying goes, "Shoot for the moon. If you fall short, you will still land among the stars."

My financial desires didn't align with my actions. I spent money at a rate that would make me part of the negative statistics. I wanted to build wealth, but I didn't take the time to understand the process of wealth building. I look back on my career and clearly see my development in understanding and building wealth.

You must develop an idea of your ideal investment picture. You must understand what you want to invest in and if those investments make sense for your portfolio, the risks and rewards that are involved, and the strategies that will be used to secure your future. It's a hundred times easier to sit down and map out a solid plan for building your future when there is significant income flow than when your professional career is over and you've used money at a rate that has exceeded your current ROI (return on investments).

Game Rule #18
Don't put all your eggs in one basket.

The sad fact is that 80 percent of athletes wait until the end of their career to plan their future. They have to spend time trying to dig themselves out of a hole rather than transitioning into their future. It's easy to deflect the blame toward someone else. But how do you blame someone else if you give him the keys to your car and allow him to drive it? You can't claim that you were carjacked when you gave away the keys and even filled the gas tank.

There are definitely some bad financial advisers in the business, but you must address the source before you attack everything that is attached to the source. The Bible states clearly, "My people perish for lack of knowledge." At the end of the day, if you throw all your eggs into one basket and you don't even fully understand what you're getting into, the result is inevitable.

The fact is, "snakes" slither around and prey on gullible athletes. Their motives are impure from the beginning. Each new client/victim they recruit runs right into the mouth of the snake. The Bible says, "The love of money is the root to all evil." Professional athletes come into money at a very fast pace. This makes it easier for unprepared athletes to put their trust in someone who is dressed in a nice suit and says they've made money for everyone, including the pope.

Let's face it, rookie athletes are young, and a lot of them think they know it all. Everything for them is still as good as it seems. Thinking that they already have all the answers, they simply don't ask many (if any) questions; if they do, they're usually the wrong questions. As rookie athletes, we don't have a solid, mature perspective on the real world and how it functions. We move forward in our careers with the blind hope that the eggs we put in the basket are multiplying. By the time many athletes find out that their money is being smuggled from them, it's too late.

Snakes like this are all over the world. No one can say that they won't fall victim to a financial snake, because a snake is a snake for a reason. It's no coincidence that the Bible says we are supposed to be as wise as serpents. You never see snakes chasing after anything. They simply sit around as the gullible are deceived and fall right into their trap.

Game Rule #19
It takes a team to win.

Gain understanding, protect your assets to the best of your ability, and surround yourself with a financial team that will oversee and manage your money with your best interests on the top of their priority list. One of the best principles we learn in sports is that it takes a team to win. Why not apply that concept to everything you do? It may cost more to have a team, but in the long run it will be well worth it. I would rather spend a few more dollars a month to make sure my money is protected and invested wisely than discover years later that I was being robbed every month. Think about it: the thief doesn't even have to wear a mask or carry a gun as long as you are an unaware victim.

Chapter 4

The Game Face

Believe in yourself! Have faith in your abilities! Without a humble but reasonable confidence in your own powers you can't be successful or happy.
—*Norman Vincent Peale*

The Right Self-Portrait

Who you are is not based on or determined by the sport you play or played. Who you are is determined by the self-portrait you've painted in your mind. Your self-portrait is the picture that carries you through life and allows others to see your character and worth. Your self-portrait will determine where you go in life and your access to the right people and right places which at the end of the day will bring you into favorable circumstances.

If my self-portrait consists only of a football or basketball, what else do I have to offer the world? I've already put myself in a box. No one had to do it for me. If what I do determines who I am, when the game is over, my forward momentum in life also ends.

You've trained your entire life to be the best actor in a particular play. When the play is over, the actor you created must retire, and the true you must start living. The trouble arises when you allow your game face to be you and you become stuck within an act that the curtains have already come down on.

Don't place yourself in a box. You'll have enough people in your life that try to do that for you. Only you can discover your true purpose on this earth. Your purpose will help you understand your worth. Always keep in mind that your purpose is much greater than your job or career. No one can walk around blind without some sort of assistance. Your eyes are your navigation system for where you're going. When you don't understand your true self-image, you're always looking for someone to guide you in the right direction. Before you know it, you're following someone else's dreams and aspirations and still haven't discovered your own.

Game Rule #20
Life doesn't happen to you; it simply responds to you.

One of my favorite quotes is "Life is 10 percent what happens to you and 90 percent how you react to it." Part of maturing and understanding who you are is told within the context of this quote. Life doesn't happen to you; it simply responds to you. How you react to different situations determines how situations respond to you. You can't understand who you are if your circumstances determine your outlook on life.

If you make a mistake, the mistake doesn't make you a mistake. Getting bent out of shape, crying, and moping around won't do anything at all to improve the situation. I've never seen anyone cry or get depressed into a better situation.

Now, it's true that some mistakes are a lot greater than others. However, mistakes reveal the imperfections that are within *all* human beings. Don't be ashamed or embarrassed by your shortcomings, because everyone has them. Our imperfections reveal our character and who we are called to be as people. Your imperfections help you discover who you really are and your purpose on this earth.

Game Rule #21
Your imperfections help you discover who you really are and
your purpose.

The Truth about Imperfections

Life is about trial and error. The wisest people in this world didn't become wise as a result of being perfect. Actually, it's the other way around. They made the most mistakes and, through that trial and error, understand who they are and where they are going in life. I stated earlier that some mistakes are greater than others. In order for you to make a big mistake, you have to be in a position where your mistake affects more than just you.

The more people your mistake affects, the more powerful your position. At the end of the day, the greater your position or calling in life, the more calculated and precise your decisions must be. Businesses have boards and husbands have wives so the risks of decisions are minimized. The decisions are for the betterment of everyone involved, not one person's gain.

I was doing an extremely hard workout one day. One of the guys, who was also persevering through it, looked at me and said, "God has dominion over your soul, your soul has dominion over your spirit, your spirit has dominion over your mind, and your mind has dominion over your body." I looked at him like he was crazy. Then what he said really hit home, and I began to think about his words. I wasn't worried about not being able to finish the workout or anything else challenging me to rise to unknown heights, because I figured out I already possessed the mental toughness to overcome anything we would have to do. Everything you or I will ever have to overcome has already been instilled in us awaiting our own discovery.

From that statement I learned that I had the mental toughness to overcome anything that was thrown my way and the ability to be good at whatever I decided to do. I also learned that my surroundings and adversity didn't dictate who I was as a man. I understood right then that whatever I wanted to do was already in me to accomplish. Therefore, as long as my spirit (my conscience) accepted it and knew it was the right thing to do, it was up to me not to question whether I would be able to accomplish it. Once doubt crosses your mind, you limit yourself. Those limits take away your ability to change the world around you. In essence, you stop yourself. You become your own worst enemy. You willingly accept the loss.

Your True Purpose

It's vital to understand that your purpose on earth and the blessings that you've obtained are all for a purpose that is bigger than you. You can't understand who you are within a sport or a career. Your character is revealed and shaped through sports, and who you are as a person is found in the realization that a higher power created you to be something greater than your mind can fathom. When your thoughts and actions begin to align with the way God sees you, you've begun to unravel who you are and your true purpose. God has to reveal himself through people so how can God reveal himself through you without you having the correct perception of who you are.

Playing sports gives you a platform of influence. How you use that influence can lead you onto the path of discovering who you are. If you're using your influence to go against the spiritual laws and currents of life, you will eventually be humbled (as so many athletes are) and brought back to the reality that you're just a pawn in the bigger game of life. If you use your influence to coincide with God's principles and laws, who you are will be revealed through your journey. The day that platform of influence is swept from under your feet is the day you realize you have to discover who you are within the greater context of life.

God has orchestrated this universe in a way that whatever you choose to abuse or take advantage of will come back to you and use your platform to humble you. During trials and tribulations, individuals are forced to examine who they are. Some quit on life and take the easy way out. Others stand up to the challenge, realizing that because they lost touch during their career, something greater had to refocus their attention on the high points in their lives.

Game Rule #22
Balance of mind, body, and spirit is the key to uncovering who you really are.

Balance is the key to uncovering who you really are. Balance of the mind, body, and spirit is important. There must be a synergy between those three for you to thrive and have confidence in who you are. When there is an imbalance, one pulls at the other. It's no different than when you're out on the field with an injury. If your left ankle is sore, your right knee or hip eventually begins to feel sore as well, as one side of your body tries to compensate for the weakness in the other.

For athletes, the easiest task is to be strong physically and mentally, but there is a void when you don't grasp anything spiritually. You can go far physically and mentally in sports, because they are the major requirements of the game. So to unlock your full potential you can't lack physically or mentally. Many people may challenge that statement, but I challenge you to look into the careers of great players. Those who became unbalanced in their mind, body, and spirit experienced a hiccup in their career that forced them to draw on their faith to elevate their consciousness and bring them out of the dilemma.

Game Rule #23
Who you are is bigger than what you do.

Physical and mental principles are key in sports, but spiritual principles have a lock on how this world flows and operates. A balance helps you realize that you can have a passion and a love for the sport, but your passion and love is not derived from the sport. Who you are is much bigger than what you do. Your purpose is bigger than you.

Who you are as a person can be discovered and solidified only by you; it is reinforced by someone else. Another person can tell you who he thinks you are or who you are supposed to be, but if you don't know for yourself, the words fall on deaf ears. So many people go through their careers not knowing and not having to know who they are. Their title defines them, and their job portrays them. That's why many athletes are lost when their careers end. They're stuck in the talent that catapulted them to a high level of the game. Forgotten are the many talents that led them to prevail in life.

If you've been successful at everything your entire life, and sports is just a small part of that, don't allow those talents to be lost when your career is over. Allow the game to be a platform to showcase all your talents and who you are. Don't get sucked into the norm and allow the game to make you the sacrifice. Why go through years of physical and mental sacrifice and come out with nothing?

A large percentage of the game is mental. Character is learned, instilled, and revealed over time. You've gone through a portion of your life excelling through mental and physical mayhem in your sports arena, so you've found out who you are at some point already. The question is, did you listen?

Chapter 5

What Happens When the Act Is Over?

You are never too old to set another goal or to dream a new dream.
—C. S. Lewis

Facing the Question

One of the most crucial questions that you ask yourself when your career has run its course and you wake up in the morning is "What do I do now?" This question confronts some people sooner than others. It's often overlooked because of an insistence that the game is not over until you say it is. "What do I do now?" a question that must be confronted and answered eventually.

Pride is a dominant force that helped get you to the level of success that you've achieved. While pride can help you along the road to success, it can also be a blinding factor that hinders your future success. The faster you pay attention to this question when it comes to your mind, the easier you will transition into your new game of life.

Your career may not be over; you may get another chance. If that's the case, take the break in action as a sign that your career is closer to the end than the beginning. Allow yourself the ability to prepare for the rest of your life, instead of missing out on a future that may have bigger opportunities in store for you.

Game Rule #24
When your focus is on what you can get out of a job as opposed to what you can bring to the table, you're setting yourself up to remain stagnant.

"What do I do now?" may be one of the most difficult questions you have ever had to face, if you're able to face it at all. You may not be ready to answer that question because you don't think you're ready for your athletic career to end. The question implies that there has to be closure to the career that you've spent a large portion of your life establishing. What do I do now? What can I possibly do that will give me the satisfaction of competition and the comfort of a sizeable paycheck?

But these aren't the right questions to ask. When your focus is on what you can get out of a job as opposed to what you can bring to it, you're setting yourself up to remain stagnant. You're preparing yourself to embrace the excuses that will arise in you and tell you that your sport is all you can do to stay in the limelight and make money. The excuses shed light on the fact that you've been hypnotized by the structure that athletics has provided for you, instead of using that structure to help you progress in life in general.

Game Rule #25
The game is a business.

I was always taught that as a child you make excuses, but as a man you make a way. Life can give back only what you put into it. Nothing in life is free. A job or career is what you bring to it and make of it.

You played sports for free until you made it professionally. So ask yourself the this: When you reached your dream and began to be compensated for doing what you loved to do, did it change the way you saw your sport? Did you play only because you were getting paid for it? No! All athletes play sports because that is what they love to do. The athletes who gave up in high school are the ones whose joy in their sport diminished.

Every athlete wants to get paid what he's worth when the opportunity presents itself for a professional career. But does the money change your outlook on the game itself? I can answer that for you. No. The money brings awareness of the fact that you are now rewarded for your talents. It brings you to the realization that the game that you love to play is a business. You must mature in the reality that you are a part of a billion-dollar industry, and you must learn to treat it as such. That means that in addition to being an athlete, you're now a businessman with a lot on his plate, tremendous potential, but many potential pitfalls. When you come into agreement with this understanding, you're able to walk into your potential and avoid the pitfalls.

The Consequences of Time Wasted

A large part of knowing what to do after your sports career ends is being able to adapt to the newfound freedom outside the structure that surrounded you your entire career. This structure defined your livelihood for a large portion of your life and dictated what you were and were not able to do. Many times former professional athletes wonder what to do with all the extra time. The problem is that we as athletes were so used to having our time scheduled for us that we don't understand how valuable our time is. We live in a world of second chances, but time is one thing you can't get back. Understand the value of your time so that you aren't wasting it or allowing someone else to.

Game Rule #26
Time is valuable.

The structure that you became immune to throughout your career and subconsciously used as a foundation to maximize your time is what you should apply to your life when your sports career is over. A blueprint was established for you so you didn't waste your time. It also showed you the consequences of wasting time. The consequences may have included being unprepared for a game or failing to get into optimal physical shape during the off-season. The list can go on, but the consequences remain the same.

Wasted time usually doesn't affect your present condition. It sows seeds for lack in your future. There's a big difference between figuring out what to do and wasting time. In one you actively search for a new career and find a new passion; in the other, you just sit around and talk about what you want to do. Every time you focus on the distractions that can't make you better, you waste time. You can't allow this to become a habit, because once you've formed that habit, you have predicted your future.

"What do I do now?" is the main question that you have to answer. You have to make a decision, whatever it may be. The career path you choose to embark upon may not bring the public glory you received when playing your sport, and you shouldn't choose a career for the notoriety it can bring. Your career after sports should be one you enjoy and that drives you. When you choose something you enjoy, you can focus on what you can bring to your new career, instead of focusing on what it can bring to you.

If you find yourself pondering how much you will be seen or if you'll still receive the perks to which you're accustomed, you're falling into the trap of your ego. Your ego is a gift and a curse. It's a gift in that it eliminates the presence of fear on the playing field and a curse in that it distorts reality. Don't let the curse side of your ego strike you down at this crucial juncture. You're at a crossroads. You can't allow anything to get in your way or to jeopardize the future happiness and well-being of you and your family.

The Power of Choice

What you decide to do in your next career shouldn't jeopardize your integrity as a man. You've spent a large portion of your career directly or indirectly establishing your brand and the significance of the name on the back of your jersey. I say directly or indirectly because some people grasp that concept easier than others. Those that don't get it right away generally end up learning through their off-the-field mistakes the consequences that their decisions can have. At this point, some athletes realize that the game they've played has been a platform to establish themselves as an entity, but that entity can easily collapse and force the question "What do I do now?" to come sooner than it may have otherwise.

Game Rule #27
Make a decision, and keep moving forward.

What you decide to do next with your life and your career can't be created without your mind and your body working in correlation to achieve your next goals. It's no different than when you were in the sports arena. You couldn't make a big play from the sidelines. You still can't. On the field, if your mind isn't focused on the anticipation that your instincts provide for you, your body can't react to what's going on. They must operate in conjunction with each other in order to create the big play.

It's no different in your life after sports. Chances are your instincts have already warned you that the end of your sports career was coming. It's up to you to make sure that you're mentally prepared to answer it in a way that causes you to actively thrust yourself into your future. One way or the other, life will force you to make a decision. It will be up to you whether or not you answer that question. If you push it to the side and decide not to address it at all, you've made a decision. That decision is to sit still and eventually rot in the glory of your past.

God gives you free will to make decisions, and no one but you can rescind that ability. A decision will wait for you to address it, but time will not stand still. It's simply on the world's cycle. God created the world to adapt and evolve constantly. The funny thing is that humans are wired to do the same thing once we fully understand our true identity. Whatever you do, make sure you're always moving forward. During my football career, the coaches used to tell us all the time that we should never be going backward as a defensive player, because that means nothing good or productive is happening. That applies to life and how we must approach every element of it. Make a decision, and keep moving forward.

Third Quarter

Chapter 6

The Game Is Not Your Idol

There is no passion to be found playing small, in settling for
a life that is less than the one you are capable of living.
—*Nelson Mandela*

Letting Go of the Past

If you're sitting around reminiscing about the job you used to have or the sport you used to play, how can you determine what your next position will be in life? Finding a new love is never easy. In fact, it can be very difficult. Finding a new love requires you to release the past and keep it exactly where it is: in the past. You can use the past to catapult you into your future, but you can't allow your past to keep you stagnant in the present. Finding a new love forces you to expand your mind outside the comforts of what you once knew and into the fears of the unknown. That unknown in society is known as dating. It's impossible to find a new love if you don't date.

The longer you stay stuck in your past position in the game of life, the more dangerous you become to yourself. You're telling the universe that what you were able to do and who you became is a result of what you did and not of who you are. You're sending out the signal that the game is your source in life, which contradicts any universal law that could allow you to prosper. The world is filled with resources that we human beings have access to. When you mistake your resources as your source rather than God, you get into an instant uphill battle with the laws of the universe, leaving you wondering how and why the world is passing you by.

Game Rule #28
Whatever you focus on, you magnify.

You must keep moving forward if you want to keep up with the universe, your future, and the next chapter of your life. Where you focus your attention will determine that next chapter. Whatever you focus on you magnify. If you focus on the past, the frustrations of being released too soon from the game that you love, the mistreatment of the coaches, you will magnify the problems of your past. You will remain stuck in the past and face even greater obstacles to a brighter future. If you want to find a new love, you have to walk by faith into the unknown of your future.

Your sports career was a blessing for a season. At the end of the day, you should use it as a springboard to catapult you into your destiny. Your new love is out there waiting for you to find it and take advantage of it. Don't compromise your destiny for fear of stepping into your future. Compromise will lead you to settle for less than what you've strived for as an athlete: *greatness!*

> *All our dreams can come true, if we have the courage to pursue them.*
> Walt Disney

Your Action Is Required

Finding a new love requires action. It wasn't enough to say that you wanted to be an all-pro player or a Hall of Fame inductee. There was a lot of work required behind the scenes. When the stadiums were empty and the coaches were not in your face, telling you what to do, you acted on your dreams and goals and did the little things that maximized your talent as athlete. The little things weren't enjoyable but were necessary for you to get an edge over the next person. Those little courses of action set the foundation for who you were as an athlete and how your coaches and peers viewed you. These actions that no one sees until the harvest is reaped should motivate and inspire you to find your new love and establish yourself in your new field.

Why remain stuck in a season of your life that was supposed to help you transition into another career if you have nothing to show for it? As uncomfortable as it may be to search for a new field of life on which to play, it's a lot more comfortable than being stagnant after your sports career is over and all your resources are depleted.

Game Rule #29
Excellence comes forth as a result of discomfort.

Why not embrace the discomfort of moving into your future, instead of holding on to the glory of your past? Excellence comes forth as a result of discomfort. Seasons greatly affect the world in which we live. There are winter, spring, summer, and fall; there are rainy seasons in the rainforests; there are dry and wet seasons in the dessert.

Likewise, there are seasons in your sports career. Just as you prepare for the change from winter to spring and from summer to fall, you must learn how to prepare for and adapt to the seasons of your life. You may not like the season that's approaching, but if you aren't prepared for it, you will be engulfed by it and desperately looking for a way of escape.

Athletes are trained to live by the laws of the jungle their entire career. Every year, sometimes even more frequently, a new player comes along who is younger and prepared to compete for your starting position. If the veteran has what it takes to hold off the young rookie draft picks and free agents, he still holds his place on the throne. That doesn't mean he can relax. The young lions are sitting around waiting to capitalize on his mistakes. However, this keeps him sharp. Knowing that there are others just waiting to take his place makes him that much stronger as a competitor.

If you spiritually dissect what goes on in the jungle, you see that it may be God's way that the weak don't reproduce themselves in this world. What seems harsh at first glance makes sense on a deeper level. If the weak could continually reproduce, how much growth would we really have in this world? The seemingly harsh law of the jungle is the universe's way of making sure there is constant progress in all phases of life.

Game Rule #30
When you live in the past, you forfeit your future.

Now, on a lot less barbaric level, this is no different than the way you must go out and find your new passion. Focus your efforts on the here and now. It's not going to come to you as you sit back, holding onto the past. You will miss your opportunity if you sit in the comfort of your past instead of moving toward the discomfort of your destiny. One of my mentors always says, "Where your focus goes, your power flows." If your focus is on your past, your power and abilities are seated in your past. Being proud of your past and having fond memories of it is acceptable. However, living in the past causes you to forfeit your future.

The lion in *The Lion King* was defeated. But if he had lied around and thought about what he had, he would have rotted away and died. This simply means that the lion had to find another group to be a part of in order to flourish as the king of the jungle. In this season of your life, you have a choice to make. You can either fade away with the memories of your past, or you can go out and find a new career that allows you operate with the confidence you used to have and move forward into another season of success.

The Process

All of us have new mountains to climb and new kingdoms to build. In other words, there's something out there that we can throw ourselves into passionately and with as much gusto as we put into athletics. However, in order to find something that you love, you have to be exposed to it. What you're exposed to determines your likes and dislikes. You can't have chemistry with something unless you've been exposed to it and your mind is aware of it.

Many people walk around blind to the blessings in this world because mentally they aren't aware, and therefore they're unable to perceive it in their minds. If you're unable to perceive it in your mind, you won't recognize it when you see it with your own eyes. Your mind can project and make real only what you're aware of. What you're unaware of is not lawful spiritually for you to possess.

Game Rule #31
Failure is not an option.

This all starts with your exposure to new things, new people, and new places. As you move out of the norm of going with the flow and doing what you feel is natural and easy, you will encounter new opportunities. However, you also expose yourself to the possibility of rejection. As you begin to move with the same confidence that you had while you were in the comfort of your sports career, you will realize that the no's you hear aren't the result of failure but of timing. There's no such thing as failure, there is only feedback, as Bishop Jordan would say. You may have to go back and perfect some flaws that you have in an area that a specific position may require. Look at rejection as constructive criticism, and keep moving forward into your purpose and destiny.

As you expose yourself to new things and new opportunities, have a solid idea of what you want to accomplish, acquire, and achieve in this next chapter of your life. This is where finding your new love can get tricky. You'll need to gain an understanding of what you're looking to manifest in your future. It's not enough to say, "I want to be successful in whatever I do." What does your "whatever" consist of? You have to expose yourself to new opportunities, which requires your focus and direction. You will come across opportunities as well as distractions. Distractions can cause chaos, encouraging us either to make rash decisions or to remain balanced in who we are and to rely on our instincts. When we remain balanced, we realize that some of our greatest opportunities are presented in the midst of chaos.

Game Rule #32
In the midst of chaos, some of your greatest opportunities are presented.

Most men know what they want as soon as they see it or experience it. While you're searching for your new love, don't waste time. Time is the one commodity that you will never get back. You can search for a new career or passion as much as you want, but you will never get that time back. Your time becomes even more precious when you're operating on your own time. The more inefficient you are with your time, the less time you will have to enjoy doing what you love when the opportunity presents itself.

Game Rule #33
Clearly discern when your career has ended.

There is no formula for finding a new love, but you can take fundamental steps to ensure that you're moving toward the path of your future. First, clearly discern when your career has ended. If you can't accept the fact that your career is over and the game has used all of you that it wants, you will not be able to move forward. You have to be able to transition from what you loved into your new passion. You can't backpedal into the next season of your life.

Game Rule #34
Establish an efficient and productive way to use your time.

Second, establish an efficient and productive way to use your time. Time wasted turns into progress lost. Your progression dictates your transition into what you become. Mental progress is just as important as physical progress.

Game Rule #35
Create a plan to expose yourself to new opportunities.

Third, create a plan to expose yourself to new opportunities. If you're progressing without any sense of direction, what are you really moving toward?

Game Rule #36
Act on your plan, and avoid excuses that keep you in your comfort zone.

Finally, act on your plan, and avoid excuses that keep you in your comfort zone. Life is not a spectator sport. You may watch it go up the field, but it will not come back down to pass you again.

The universe was created to move, but it doesn't sway back and forth. The currents of the universe are distinct and flow in one constant direction. Whether or not you're able to move with the currents of life determines your success or failure. You are the architect of your future. The blueprint that you design for your transition becomes the structure for your future. Your ability to progress and open yourself to new opportunities becomes the material you use to build your future.

Chapter 7

Your New Stadium

I feel like I have a new life, and I'm going to take full advantage of it.
—*William Green*

What You See Is What You Get

Your new stadium of life can be as big as you allow it to be. Where you see yourself going in your new career determines the size of the stadium in which you will play. The biggest stadiums usually have the teams that are most successful, and those teams are seen and recognized by a lot more people.

Your purpose in your new phase of life is not to please others. Your outlook on where you're going will determine how others look at you. Promotion doesn't come through negativity.

Game Rule #37
Promotion is the direct result of consistency and expectation.

Promotion is the direct result of consistency and expectation. Consistency in your actions makes you reliable. Your expectations send out the signal that you understand what you want to achieve and where you want to go. You must take your new stadium by force—not the physical brute force that we as athletes all think we have, but with the expectations you need in order to know where and what you need to do to grow to be the big fish in your stadium of destiny.

This is the point in your life where you must transition from the assumption that you can get by on your physical talent alone. You don't have to run up and down the field anymore. You have to allow your mind to come to the forefront so you can establish the same savvy your body exhibited in your sport. Most of us forget that we were not robots while we were playing sports. We simply received instructions, and from those instructions our minds had to dictate to our bodies what to do and how to succeed.

Practice prepared you for the game, which enhanced your awareness. The foundation of what you were able to perform started in your mind and in the limitless goals you set for yourself to achieve while you were on the field. Your mind got you to where you were in life. Your body just brought you to the destination that was set in your mind. As an athlete, you were brilliant. You were always a great thinker.

But at some point, almost all of us allowed the illusions of this world to convince us that our physical prowess was the reason for our success on the field. Your mind is the true stadium of your life. When you set limits in your mind of what you're able to accomplish, they have the potential to dictate the size of the stadium that you will dwell in for the rest of your life.

Game Rule #38
You determine what you're going to accomplish next in life.

Your new stadium should be easy to find, but it's not. Why? The reason may surprise you. Athletes are accustomed to thinking of life in an external sense. We travel from city to city. We become part of a team and participate in all the activities. We interact with fans and others who support us. All of those things are wonderful, and they have their place in the game. But that isn't what I mean when I refer to a new stadium. Your new stadium isn't out in the world. It's in the depths and intricacies of your mind.

You determine what you're going to accomplish next. Your stadium can be the Big House of the University of Michigan and fit more than 110,000 people in it, or it can be a small high school stadium that allows you to take advantage of your niche market. Just make sure you aren't the one constantly complaining that you don't have a stadium to play in. That only reflects on you as a person.

You also don't want to be the one who creates the big stadium but it's empty because you're busy doing what your ego wants to do and not what you're called to do. When you don't have a stadium to play in, you're always looking for someone to lend you his or her stadium so you fit in and are a part of something. But you weren't created to feed off someone else's vision. As long as you're running around without an understanding of what you want to do, you will not believe that you can be the best for yourself. You'll focus your energy on trying to be the best for someone else, which will result in your paying rent to use his or her property. Most definitely, that is not what you want!

Game Rule #39
Creativity is a gift.

Get to know the real you, and allow the unlimited resources of your mind to create and establish your own stadium, which will be a light for others. Do you realize the incredible opportunities you have right at your fingertips? The limits are literally the limits of your imagination, which is infinite.

Creativity is a gift. Now you're able to exercise it and utilize it to its fullest. The deeper you dig, the more amazing the treasure you will find. It's like diamonds buried deep inside of a mine and hidden from the outside world until a courageous miner goes down and brings them up to the surface. That's how you should envision the building of your incredible stadium from the inside out. Create it from the richest materials in the universe: the thoughts of your own mind.

Mind Power

You might be in danger of creating a stadium that can't support what you want to do or where you want to go. This can happen when you don't submit to the inner you that guided you in making the big plays of your past. It's a result of operating outside of the will of a higher power. And you end up putting a basketball court in a football stadium or a baseball field in a basketball stadium. It doesn't fit, and because it doesn't fit, nobody wants to come to see you play. The result is a big stadium that you can't maintain because your distorted vision doesn't support the structure you tried to create. It's not a pretty picture, and you should avoid it at all costs.

Game Rule #40
You are a co-creator with God of your world.

You have probably heard the saying "A mind is a terrible thing to waste." There is great wisdom in that sublime statement. You can't fully appreciate the depth of it until you understand the power of your mind. When you grasp the truth that your mind gives you the power to create your own truth in this world, you can begin to grasp the concept at the heart of that statement.

To accomplish anything in life, you have to be able to see yourself doing it first in spirit. You have to be able to believe that you can accomplish a specific goal before your mind even allows your body to attempt it physically. God gave you the power to think. Therefore, you and God are co-creator of your world.

Now, some people may object, saying, "But how can that be? I can't control everything that happens to me!" That is true. You may not be in control of every situation, but you are in control of your reactions. That is real power, especially if you're able to put all of this power into proper perspective. Your mind is your passport to the physical manifestation of your success. What you're able to comprehend in your mind establishes your reality in the physical world.

Game Rule #41
Don't allow someone's truth to become your reality.

People who allow limitations to dictate their lives are often the main force attempting to control what you can and can't achieve in your reality. Therefore, you must know and understand the miracle of you. Walking around with a true understanding of the miracle of you on this earth will allow you to smile at those who wish to hinder your reality with the truths of their world and to keep you from reaching for the dreams you know will become your reality.

When you're lost in your mind, you will also lose tangible goods. If you question yourself on the inside, you will lack confidence on the outside. Whatever you go through internally, you reflect externally in your world.

Be Careful of Your Thoughts

Your new stadium is the culmination of the thoughts that comprise your physical presentation to the rest of the world. You constantly carry around the stadium that you create for yourself. Every time you dwell on the past or bask in what you *could* have done, you give a poor performance for your audience. Generally, people only want to see and support winners. Therefore, when you aren't striving toward the greatness inside of you, you walk alone. Paul Morton said that being average is being on the top of the losers. When you're just getting by and coasting through life, the most you can allow yourself to be is the captain of the underachievers.

Game Rule #42
Your thoughts are magnified in your outside world.

You've probably noticed that those with great ambition think positively. They're used to their stadiums being sold out and having crowds of onlookers watch as they reach for their goals.

Opportunities seem to come to them not because they are better but because they think on a higher level. As a result, more people are interested in what they're doing. Pessimistic people always seem to point out the negative in others, probably because they can't find the positive in themselves. You can always find seats in their stadiums, because they're usually empty.

Your thoughts are magnified in your outside world. If you think positive thoughts, you magnify positivity around you. If you think negative thoughts, you magnify negativity around you. Countless books and studies have been published proving this very fact. But you don't need to read them. You can simply test it in your own life. Clearly, we were designed that way, very purposefully. The ability to control your mind and your thoughts is paramount to what and who you attract into your stadium of life.

This universal law can't be changed, so why fight it, especially when it works to your benefit if you adhere to its principles? I'm not saying that you can merely think your way into positive results. I'm saying that it all begins with your mind. Your thoughts set in motion all that is to follow. All of the good things that can come your way and the positive energy that you can share with others begin inside you with your rightly focused, positive thoughts. In a sense, everything else is about filling in the details.

It's easy to control your thoughts when everything is going in your favor and you feel like you're on top of the world. However, what happens when things aren't going your way, when it seems like nothing you do is working and doors aren't opening like they used to? This is when you can reveal yourself to yourself. This is when your mind can become a war zone and you have to conquer your own negative perceptions in order to find the confidence that put you on top of the world. It's funny how people say that they are not perfect and at the same time find it so hard to forgive themselves over their imperfections. Maybe you have made a mistake, but surely it's not the first, and it's definitely not the last.

Game Rule #43
Your stadium is established by understanding your talents and your purpose.

When you're able to stand strong in who you are and to control your thought process even through the down times, you've just solidified your stadium and your franchise in life. Instead of looking at every situation and saying, "Judas betrayed me," you can look deeper and say, "Thank you, Judas, for carrying out your mission to push me toward my purpose and my destiny." Not everyone will understand that statement, but know that I am not speaking death on anyone. Jesus's purpose and calling was to die to save many, and what Judas did ushered Him toward the mandate over His life. When you understand your purpose on this earth, it's easier to discern other people's purpose in your life. Some of the biggest opportunities are missed when we try to use people for a different purpose than what they are called to in our lives.

Make sure that you do everything in your power to establish your stadium. It's easy to overlook things if you fail to pay attention to detail. Remember, your stadium is established by understanding your talents and your purpose. When you understand these, you realize that everything is not about you; there is a whole world of people waiting for what you have to offer. A major aspect of your purpose is to utilize your talents to make people around you better. What a great incentive to get out there and shine!

Imagine the satisfaction you will feel as you take advantage of the terrific opportunities to help others that present themselves to you. Think of times in the past when someone helped you. Do you recall how grateful you were? Chances are that person who shared something valuable with you probably felt even better than you felt. This biblical principle still holds true: "It is better to give than to receive." What can compare to being a blessing to a fellow human being?

No matter what stage you're in, someone can learn from you, and you can learn from someone. This is the way the universe was made. Through giving and receiving, human beings are able to manifest into their true greatness. Wherever a talented person is all about self-gratification and only cares about himself, there is a form of rebellion around him. Every great player can make people around him better. That's true for any athlete, political leader, spiritual leader, or any other human being who is placed in a leadership position.

Game Rule #44
Greatness breeds greatness.

Think of people you admire. It's not all about them, is it? Of course not. The universe is established on giving and receiving, sowing and reaping. Whenever you go against a universal law, you lose at the end of the day. You can't grow within yourself until you fully understand these principles. A tree is known from the fruit it bears. Your stadium is established through the people you learn from and the people you influence. You always see great athletes of the present paying homage to great athletes of the past that they learned different aspects of their game From.

Greatness breeds greatness. Iron sharpens iron. The stadium that you establish for yourself is your platform to share your talents. It is also a place where you're able to sharpen your talents.

Keep the right mind-set. Your attitude is like the grounds crew for your stadium. When your attitude is off, the field or the court inside your stadium isn't up to playing standards. A game can't be played inside that stadium until the grounds are in perfect condition.

Fourth Quarter

Chapter 8

Conquering on Your New Home Turf

*I've missed more than nine thousand shots in my career. I've lost
almost three hundred games. Twenty-six times I've been trusted
to take the game-winning shot and missed. I've failed over and
over and over again in my life. And that is why I succeed.*
—*Michael Jordan*

The Power Is in Your Hands

You will establish your new home turf only after you learn
how to build the stadium in your mind. Once you've learned how to
develop a solid foundation for your stadium, you'll be able to move
forward and conquer anything that tries to disturb your faith in who
and what you are. In essence, you have to conquer your thoughts
and understand that you are the sum of your thoughts. Building
your stadium begins from you understanding that your mind and
your thoughts are your world.

Game Rule #45
You are the sum total of your thoughts.

To claim your stadium as your home turf is to be able to
dictate and control your thoughts. No one and nothing can come
into your house and determine your mood and outlook for any

given day. A quote often attributed to Mahatma Gandhi reads, "I will not let anyone walk through my mind with their dirty feet." That one sentence says that nothing and no one will defeat me on my home field or court. I am building this stadium, and I take pride in defending what I have established.

Conquering your home turf is not about building your stadium of life; it's about maintaining your stadium and establishing your brand in the world. To get something is one thing, and it may seem like an exhausting process at times. To establish and maintain it is the true process and the most difficult race to run. The marathon of life involves maintaining a positive outlook and understanding the power of your mind. Don't allow negative circumstances to create questions regarding who you've become, but allow them to strengthen you to overcome any obstacle that life presents to you.

Once you know who you are and what you stand for, what can block your path? You will be unstoppable. As long as your purpose is just and includes the good of others, you will be proud of the magnificent stadium that you've built, and you'll defend that home turf with every fiber of your being.

Conquering Your Fears

Many people are unable to establish their new home turf. Contrary to popular belief, establishing your turf has nothing to do with the amount of money you accumulate. It has everything to do with how you control your mental atmosphere. Money can build a stadium, but it can't establish the stadium's foundation. That is something personal that only you can do. The creation that ultimately unfolds will be more unique than a fingerprint or even a strand of DNA. We are literally talking about what is inside you: your spirit, which makes up who you are.

Game Rule #46
Money can build a stadium, but it can't establish the stadium's foundation.

Many wealthy people are empty on the inside and can't figure out who they are. It has been said that some people are so rich they are poor. Money allows access and freedom of choice, but it is not a solid foundation on which to stand. The foundation is the character you've built within yourself over the years in order to stand strong in who you are today.

Your character allows you to maintain your new stadium. It leaves you confident in who you are, no matter what circumstance life throws your way. It's easy to operate in confidence when everything is going according to plan. The key is to be able to function in the same spirit of peace and excellence during the most difficult and trying times. This is what separates those who are simply aware of who they have become and those who have developed an understanding and a faith in who they truly are. Life is full of ups and downs, no matter who you are and where you are in your life. The key is to roll with the punches in order to maintain the core balance and not get lost in the process.

We human beings are designed to have one of two reactions when adverse situations present themselves: fight or flight. The process of life is all about reaching and achieving your goals, but there is a fight within that process. The process of achieving your goals is the training ground for maintaining and developing what you have. If you talk to any great boxer or boxing coach, he or she will say that when a person first gets into the ring to learn how to fight, when he sees a punch coming, he steps straight back. His reflexes tell him that as long as he goes backward, he will be safely out of the way of the punch.

The problem is that now he has gotten himself out of position and in line to be hit by more punches than the one that he saw coming. What seemed safe and the right thing to do was actually the most dangerous thing to do. The art of boxing is to be able to be in the proper fighting position and to be able to stay in the range (pocket) of where your mind is saying you aren't safe and you're going to get hit. You need to be relaxed so you can slip out of the way of the punch coming at you. By simply slipping to one side or the other to avoid the punch, you maintain your proper position and are able to fight back.

Game Rule #47
You must conquer your fears and push forward in order to reach your destiny.

This same principle holds true for a woman in the delivery room having a baby. When the pains of labor begin, the natural reaction is to tense up, which is the mind's way of running from the pain. The true fight is when the doctor comes in during the most painful and trying time of the delivery process and says the exact opposite of what her mind is telling her body to do: "I need you to relax and push."

In the scariest and most difficult times, we must fall back on the lessons we've been taught and that have been proven, tried, and tested. You must conquer your fears and push forward in order to reach your destiny.

In football, boxing, or a delivery room, most see the external process and miss the spiritual laws that are revealed through them. The training camp that the fighter goes through establishes his character and teaches him what he needs to do to be victorious in a fight. What was developed during training camp allows him to persevere throughout a tough fight and win a victory. It's inevitable that during the fight each fighter is going to get hit with at least one punch. The harder the punch, the more questions are created in the fighter's mind.

No Pain, No Gain

What separates the great fighters from the average fighters is their ability to adjust to the mistakes they made and to stick to the game plan developed during training. Victories over our adversities come as we focus and don't give in to the flight mentality, which really means running from the character that we've developed over the course of our lives. Victories come from staying in character and conquering the fear of adversity, being able to avoid punches while watching your opponent miss, and staying relaxed so you can press forward into your destiny. This is what allows us human beings to maintain all the benefits of our hard work.

You must stay focused and conquer your fears. The greatest opponent you have in life often dwells in your own head. Until you're able to conquer the myth of yourself, you're unable to claim your home field. You have to be able to control your thoughts consistently, or someone else can easily come in and dictate your position.

Game Rule #48
You must defeat the illusions you've created.

A powerful spiritual leader once told me a story of a man who was having nightmares every night. He dreamed of a big monster chasing him. He would run and run and run until he would finally wake up. Then he'd feel safe, as if he had actually escaped. One night, while dreaming that dream, he decided he had run enough and was not going to run anymore. He stopped, turned around, faced the monster, and said, "What do you want?" The monster stopped, looked at him, and said, "I don't know. You tell me. It's your dream."

The young man had to take a stand to realize that what he was running from was the giant that he'd created in his own mind. He had to defeat the illusion he had created in order to establish his own peace. At that very point, he was given the key to conquering his home turf. The consistency with which you use that key to your mind to control your world and maintain your power will determine if you're able to establish your home turf. The alternative is to submit to the obstacles and adversities of life that are actually a part of the process of strengthening you.

In sports, the other team always tries to attack your weakest point. Either you use this opportunity to get stronger or you fall apart and fall victim to the flight mentality. One purpose of taking tests in school is to reveal a students' weaknesses and address them. If those weaknesses are ignored, the student falls behind. When your body is sore, the doctor has to expose the source of the weakness so you can get help to function normally.

Game Rule #49
Winning is an attitude.

Winning is an instilled attitude. You have to be the best person that you were born to be. This is something only you can do through understanding the magnitude of how great you were created to be. As long as you do the best that you can with the greatest picture you can portray of yourself, you are essentially winning.

But how do you react when you don't win? A true winner doesn't like losing, but at the same time he learns from that experience and comes back stronger. A loser takes a loss at face value and blames someone instead of looking at the situation as an opportunity to learn and grow.

Make sure your attitude is always set to being a winner in life. How can you ever reach your full potential and live out your purpose if your attitude isn't set on winning in the game of life?

Chapter 9

The Final Whistle

You are a vessel used by God to accomplish a greater purpose in life.
—Victor Hobson

Many factors contribute to the maturity and evolution of an athlete. My testimony is what I've been through as an athlete and as a human being on this earth, the trials and tribulations that I've learned from and am able to draw from in order to guide someone else in the right direction.

I was once a statistic. I was stuck holding on to my game face and couldn't find a way to take on the face of life. I was enmeshed in the sport I was playing before I could reach out and find the man I am today. I was looking for a stadium of life in which to play but rented ones owned by others because I was searching for my true purpose.

I now stand as an overcomer with a solid understanding of who I am in God and who God is in me. I stand as the harvest of the seeds of greatness that were planted in my life by my parents, grandparents, wife, mentors, coaches, and spiritual advisers, and nothing and no one can convince me of anything different. We are all vessels being used by God to accomplish a greater purpose. You discover your purpose through continual growth and through greater understanding who you are and the balance between your mind, body, and spirit.

Everyone is a product of his or her environment. Your environment plays a large part in shaping your character. You decide whether you will allow the character that your environment has developed to determine what you become or to use the character that has been developed to create the world around you. This choice is a fact of life. But one of those choices will limit the person you are and can become.

Prepare yourself for the position in life that you desire so that when it comes suddenly, like a gust of wind, you aren't looking around, trying to figure out how to maintain your position once you get it. Your preparation is what leads to your sustainability. Many athletes want to be starters on the team but fail to prepare like starters. Many people want to be millionaires but don't plan for wealth. As a result, when the opportunity presents itself, they aren't ready. You can't have your past attitude and expect to seize your future. You must prepare for whatever you ask for, even when there isn't the slightest sign of it.

Game Rule #50
What you lose physically, you should double mentally.

Don't allow yourself to be underprepared. Take the steps to make sure you get better with age. Don't fall into the illusion the league creates—that you get worse as you get older—because you will carry that lie with you into your future. What you lose physically, you should double mentally. Your mental maturity will allow you to dictate your world and control your future.

Everything you go through is a part of the process that prepares you for your destiny: the uncomfortable moments of being released from a team for the first time, being forced to discover your true self separate from what your profession made you, and learning how to conquer the self-defeating mentalities that leave you standing still in a constantly moving world. Your process is your testimony for where you're going. Some people have had a very difficult process to get where they are, so never judge someone's harvest without fully understanding his seed. Life is a journey, and the process is with you over the course of your walk.

I will never regret anything in my life, but my reactions to different situations had a lot to do with whether or not I made certain situations more difficult. How I reacted to instructions determined whether or not I got in trouble or lost something. How I reacted to authority determined whether I was ready to step into a position of authority. If you can't submit to authority, you can't operate in authority. How I reacted to adversity determined whether or not I could overcome the situation right away. A person's reactions have a greater effect on his overall success than you might expect.

Game Rule #51
Never judge someone's harvest without fully understanding his seed.

An in-depth analysis will allow you to see that where you are right now has a lot to do with who you did or didn't listen to. The universe is based on the law of giving and receiving and doesn't allow for deviation from that principle. One of the most fundamental principles from the beginning of time is the foundation of your growth as a human being.

Let's talk about divorcing the game. When you hear the word *divorce,* do you immediately think of hurt, pain, sadness, disappointment, and heartache? While all of these emotions are valid and real when you leave the game that you love and have devoted your life to, the most important accomplishment is discovering who you are and your ultimate purpose on earth. You have to divorce anything that can stop you from moving forward. You have to see setbacks as stepping-stones, defeats as opportunities to win on a greater scale, and adversities as weights to strengthen you. You have to divorce yourself from the shackles that hold you back.

You have to dismantle the limiting thoughts and defeatist mentality that will keep you stagnant and hoping that you'll see your next sports breakthrough on the horizon. You have to realize that the reason you can't move forward is not because of the hurt or because of the pain but because you aren't aware of your greatness. You aren't aware of who you really are. You have to divorce yourself from everything that appears to have shackled your progress and blocked you from moving forward. I woke up one morning and said, "If I don't divorce myself from this, I will never move forward."

There is no perfect being. Yet you can't fail at anything; "failure" is just feedback that pushes you toward your potential. Whatever you put your mind to, you're able to achieve. If you weren't able to focus and achieve greatness, you wouldn't have reached your level of success, whether it's playing football, attending a university to get drafted, or doing whatever you did to begin your professional sports career.

Your playing career's end does not equal failure. It actually equals transition, and transition equals success. As long as you're in transition, you still have traction you're still moving forward. As long as you're moving forward, you're going to meet new opportunities and new possibilities. You have to find opportunities in what looks like struggle. You have to embrace the grind.

Giving up is not an option. You're done playing or you're forced to divorce the game, but that doesn't mean you're giving up. You're moving on. There's power in moving on. Affirm within yourself, "I am not giving up. I am moving on."

You have to be determined to fight and go after what is yours. Take hold of your success. Grasp the greatness in you, and build a new stadium that will be a blessing to others. Nothing that is great, nothing that is worth having, comes without a fight. There is inherent greatness in you. See and feel the greatness, and fight to get there.

If you fall behind, run faster. Never give up, never
surrender, and rise up against the odds.
—Jesse Jackson

SEVEN DAYS OF AWARENESS

This is your opportunity to document your journey through the understanding of who you are as you unravel your true purpose on this earth. For seven days in each quarter you are able to focus on the principles that you have discovered throughout the book. Write down your game plan notes and analyze them as you prepare to take on your new found purpose in life. You are no longer defined by what you played, you now define what you played and/or what you do by who you have allowed yourself to see you truly are. Map out your plan and prepare to take hold of your destiny.

First Quarter
Game Plan Notes

Who Am I?

As you become more clear about who you really are, you'll be able to decide what is best for you—the first time around.
—Oprah Winfrey

Day 2

Day 3

Day 4

Day 5

Day 6

Day 7

Second Quarter
Game Plan Notes

Develop Your Infrastructure

You can't build a great building on a weak foundation. You must have a solid foundation if you're going to have a strong superstructure.
—*Gordon B. Hinckley*

Day 2

Day 3

Day 4

Day 5

Day 6

Day 7

Third Quarter
Game Plan Notes

Control your destiny

> *You may not control all the events that happen to you,*
> *but you can decide not to be reduced by them.*
> —*Maya Angelou*

Day 2

Day 3

Day 4

Day 5

Day 6

Day 7

Fourth Quarter
Game Plan Notes

The Champion revealed in you

A true champion will fight through anything.
—Floyd Mayweather Jr.

Self-awareness is probably the most important thing toward being a champion.
—Billie Jean King

Day 2

Day3

Day 4

Day 5

Day 6

Day 7

TRUE DIRECTIONS
An affiliate of Tarcher Perigee

OUR MISSION

Tarcher Perigee's mission has always been to publish
books that contain great ideas. Why? Because:

GREAT LIVES BEGIN WITH GREAT IDEAS

At Tarcher Perigee, we recognize that many talented authors,
speakers, educators, and thought-leaders share this mission
and deserve to be published – many more than Tarcher Perigee
can reasonably publish ourselves. True Directions is ideal for
authors and books that increase awareness, raise consciousness,
and inspire others to live their ideals and passions.

Like Tarcher Perigee, True Directions books are designed to do three things:
inspire, inform, and motivate.

Thus, True Directions is an ideal way for these important voices to
bring their messages of hope, healing, and help to the world.

Every book published by True Directions– whether it is non-
fiction, memoir, novel, poetry or children's book – continues
Tarcher Perigee's mission to publish works that bring positive
change in the world. We invite you to join our mission.

For more information, see the True Directions website:

www.iUniverse.com/TrueDirections/SignUp

Be a part of Tarcher Perigee's community to bring positive change in this
world! See exclusive author videos, discover new and exciting books, learn
about upcoming events, connect with author blogs and websites, and more!
www.tarcherbooks.com

TRUE DIRECTIONS
AN AFFILIATE OF TARCHER PERIGEE